Stuff About Writing, Writing About Stuff

Writing advice that actually works! Tips from a top published author, plus useful stuff to try.

Alan Dapré

Lello Dug Publishing

Cover design: Alan Dapré

Printed in the United Kingdom

www.alandapre.com

Contents

Introduction 1

1. Reasons for Writing 4
      For Yourself
      For Enjoyment
      For Others
      To Sell
      For Fame
      For Empowerment

2. The Writing Process 11
      Write from Experience
      Know Your Audience
      Meet Experienced Authors
      Write across Genres
      When to Write?

How to Stay Fresh
Avoiding Distractions

3. Stuff About Stories   21
     What is a Story?
     Story Premise and Theme
     Story Arcs
     Story Titles
     Story Focus
     Story Development
     Story Action
     Story Reaction
     Story Consequences

4. Deeper Stuff   32
     Conflict
     Problem to Fix
     Emotional Connections

5. Four Story Types   36
     Born Again Story
     Disruption Story
     Journey Story
     Question Story

6. Generating Narratives   43

7. Creating Characters   45
     Character characteristics

Stereotypes

Character names

8. Settings   51
    In the mood
    Static or Dynamic
    Real or Imagined

9. Stuff about Plots   57
    Plot and Structure
    Drama and Plot
    Subplots
    Subplots and Exposition

10. Stuff about Twists   64
     Twisting Plots
     Shocking Twists
     Revelatory Twists

11. Cliffhangers   69

12. Exploring Your Style   72
     Finding a Voice
     Finding Truth
     Finding Respect
     Finding Variety
     Finding the Right Recipe

13. Stuff that Works   81
     Know the Audience

If It Feels Wrong It Usually Is
Be Like Spock
Play with Expectations
Show Don't Tell
Reappraise Rejection
Better Than It Was
Clarity is Everything
Value Your Name
Rule of Three

14. Writing Prompts   98
First and Last
Senses
Signs
Conversations
News
Unexpected Incidents
First Lines
Photographs
Memories

15. Summing Up All That Stuff   110
Selected Works by Alan Dapré

Introduction

> 'Dad, lots of social media influencers give out writing tips. They don't have your experience. You should write a book about stuff that actually works!' - Isla

Good advice from my teenage daughter. After all, I had been scribbling down plenty of tips and writing-related thoughts over the years. Maybe it was time to gather stuff together?

Sixty-one picture and chapter books traditionally published for children and teenagers. Several stage plays. A bunch of broadcast BBC Radio plays, plus a hundred or so television scripts transmitted worldwide. I've been busy, even though I'm far from being a household name. I prefer to let my writing take the credit.

See this book as a handy tool for starting out on a professional path. More established writers may wish to remind themselves of things they have forgotten. Nothing is set in stone. It's just writing-related stuff that works for me. Each chapter has a broad theme, typically broken down into smaller elements. You can explore each element via a set of stuff to try. There are also quotes to give context and inspire and motivate.

I sent proof copies to a range of writers. Jackie Kay CBE - who was Scotland's Makar and is also an award winning novelist, prolific children's author Vivian French MBE, and Roald Dahl Funny Prize winning author - Philip Ardagh. Here's what they think.

'Jam packed with interesting quotes from other writers and thinkers, plus tips and ideas to help get your creative juices flowing, Stuff About Writing, Writing About Stuff is a handy handbook for new writers in need of prompts and ideas. But it is also a fabulous tool for experienced writers who have run out of juice. Alan Dapre turned to writing as a child growing up in a Care Home and it saved him. Writing, as he explores here, is not just for pleasure, but also key to survival. A generous and thoughtful handbook that can be any writer's trusty companion through the long and sometimes lonely hours ahead.'
- Jackie Kay

'This is THE essential book for anyone interested in writing for children. There's a wealth of useful information, helpful tips, good sense and encouragement from a children's book author who absolutely knows what

he's talking about. It's written with wonderful warmth and enthusiasm ... every potential writer should have a copy!'
- Vivian French

The most readable book about writing I've ever read, Alan Dapré's STUFF ABOUT WRITING shows why he's been such a successful writer of children's books, stage & radio plays and TV scripts. It's full of instantly accessible suggestions, ideas and observations, with plenty of wriggle room for different types of writers and would-be writers to take their own path. The whole thing is written in such a seemingly simple style – the mark of a good 'how-to' writer – that it's easy to overlook just how good the advice is, from common sense to advice honed and polished over years of publication and performance. I thoroughly recommend it.
- Philip Ardagh

The key to professional writing is to write as much as you can, when you can, as best you can.

See this book as a springboard, a smorgasbord or ... an ironing board that will help you write more smoothly.

Happy writing!

'Why be ordinary when you can be extraordinary?' - Alan Dapré

Reasons for Writing

For Yourself

The first draft of any story is For My Eyes Only, so I never have to worry about what anyone else may think. This subjective approach helps me to relax and concentrate on the essential elements of the story.

There are enough thoughts going around a writer's head without having to worry about what other people might think. If writers are disinterested it will show on the page. Write with enough passion.

Not having to impress others is a great thing. If you are hoping to have your work published, it makes sense to initially keep external critics at bay while you learn to master your internal one.

Stuff to try

- Having an emotional connection is important. Write about a subject you passionately love.

- Or write about one you actively dislike.

- Write about a secret that is a burden.

- Write boldly about a fear or hope for the future.

'Better to write for yourself and have no public, than to write for the public and have no self.' - Cyril Connolly

For Enjoyment

It is tempting, though distracting, to see what other writers are doing.

Be happy for them but focus more on enjoying your writing.

The only important writer is you!

If the writing process becomes a slog, build in days when you play with words and write just for fun.

Enjoyment is key. Though we all have tough days where words do not flow, where the creative muse has left us with a blank page.

The more you enjoy seeing your words on the page, the more likely your readers will too.

Stuff to try

- Reflect on how you feel about other writers. Is it all positive? If not, consider why.

- Focus on yourself. Write about an emotional memory that has deep meaning for you.

- My favourite sounding words are obfuscated and defenestration. My least is lorry. What words do you enjoy saying (or not)?

'Find a subject you care about and which you, in your heart, feel others should care about.' - Stephen King

For Others

Writing words for other people to read can be daunting. It is never easy to work out what is taking place inside someone else's head, so I find it easiest to start from what is inside mine.

I always begin with a story that I want to tell. The best, most engaging, story I have. A story so interesting that someone - somewhere - will want to read it.

Of course, the hard part is teasing it out of the imagination and onto the page. Every story begins with just one word. That's all.

Begin.

Stuff to try

- Read a favourite story and consider its attractions. Was it the strong characterisation, a pacy plot or a satisfying ending?

- Take a single word - such as friendship, fear, rejection or peace - and make it link to a personal experience so it is meaningful for you.

- Observe people as you go about your day and reflect on the nature of stories they might want to read.

'A bird doesn't sing because it has an answer, it sings because it has a song.' - Maya Angelou

To Sell

Agents, publishers, editors and marketing teams know what it takes to sell a book. A lot of time and money. So they seek out stories they hope readers will buy.

Whenever a book becomes a bestseller, imitations follow. But there is no point trying to jump on a bandwagon, because by the time you see one it is already disappearing into the distance!

Better to write well-rounded characters into a memorable setting and give them dynamic and interesting conflicts to solve. Fully engage your characters and you will fully engage your readers.

Keep in mind that what you see on the shelves was created a while ago.

Stuff to try

- Read books in your chosen market.

- Pick a few publishers and see if you can identify each one's house style.

- See if you can detect a trend going on in bookshops. Popular themes involving vampires, zombies, pirates, etc.

- Every genre has a formula. Explore book clichés.

'The freelance writer is a man who is paid per piece or per word or perhaps.' - Robert Benchley

For Fame

Some authors say fame can bring financial security and stability, leading to more relaxed writing. Others say the worse thing authors can do is chase fame because, inevitably, their writing will suffer.

It is true many celebrity authors have an advantage. Huge fan bases packed with people ready to buy the brand building book, regardless of quality. It can be disheartening when celebrity books occupy acres of shelf space. Though, if the first book is bad there may not be a second.

Being ambitious is different from seeking fame. Ambition may actually motivate and give writers more confidence in their writing. My view? Write the best stories, poems or scripts that you can and let the fame thing take care of itself.

Far better to have loyal readers who appreciate you for your words, not your fame.

Stuff to try

- Gather quotes from famous writers. Analyse them for a common thread.

- Consider whether fame is really the best measure of an author's success.

- Write a short story about the upside or downside of fame.

'I wanted to be successful, not famous.' - George Harrison

For Empowerment

Maybe you are like me ... and have been writing since you were a child. Happily creating colourful stories in imaginative worlds.

If so, only you will know what drew you to this form of creative expression. I lived in a dismal children's home, where I took refuge in words and worlds. Sat in a corner, scribbling stories on scraps of paper. My fanciful ideas flowed as I let my imagination take me to faraway places.

The act of writing empowered me to take charge of my thoughts and emotions. I wrote because I had to. It gave me control and independence. Something I didn't have in the real world.

Stuff to try

- Reflect on why you (have to) write.

- Consider the triggers that motivate you to write.

- What is it about writing that you like?

- What frustrates you?

'Either write something worth reading or do something worth writing.' - Benjamin Franklin

The Writing Process

Write from Experience

My first play on BBC Radio - *Kenny* - was about two teenagers leaving the care system. A follow up play - *Stranger in the Home* - was a love affair set in an old people's home, voiced superbly by Bernard Hepton.

Both drew on memories.

Kenny riffed on my actual experiences in care, while *Stranger in the Home* was based on my recollections of older people, and how they emotionally relate to each other. I didn't need to be a teenager or old person to write these plays, I just needed to refer to relationships, incidents and people in my life.

When writing from experience it is tempting to pour emotions onto the page. Unsurprisingly, a story full of grief or anger will not engage if there is no structure or plot, or the dialogue and characters are underwritten.

So what makes a story sing?

Truthful details bring stories alive. The more truth us writers experience, the more authentic our writing becomes. Yesterday, an old woman shuffled by with a bulging plastic bag. Today, I'm still wondering what was in it.

Stuff to try

- Keep your eyes open for suitable subjects to write about; a bulging suitcase, a loose rope, a faded curtain.

- Picture a crowded train station. Describe what you see and feel when a familiar person runs towards you.

- Take an evocative memory full of emotion and rewrite it into an impassive newspaper report. Then identify those parts of the story that resonate most.

- Hold a personal possession from your childhood. Recall your thoughts when you first held it. What emotions did you experience back then? Have they changed over time?

'A writer needs three things; experience, observation, and imagination. Any two of which, at times any one of which, can supply the lack of the others.' - William Faulkner

Know Your Audience

I mainly write for children. No longer a child, I ask myself an obvious question. *'What do kids like to read these days?'*

Do I give young readers more of the same with my style thrown in, or something completely different? Children love familiarity but they also love to be surprised, as do publishers!

When I am unsure what to write, I chat to children during author visits. I also browse the children's section of my local library. You name it, I read it. I examine the style, the words, the 'voice', the presentation and the tone. This is not about copying other authors. You have to be a reader to know your readers.

Stuff to try

- Write a diary post about one day last week. Then turn the post into a longer blog, vlog - or whatever the latest online communication method is!

- Reflect on short-form and long-form ways of communicating. Consider the differing expectations of your audience.

- Take a short story and rework it into a longer one.

'The audience dictates what you do or don't change.'
- H. Fierstein

Meet Experienced Authors

Most writers are generous with advice and support, though some may be guarded, even dismissive. Take on board anything that might work for you and ignore the rest.

When you meet successful published writers always value your writing. Ensure you interact as equals. Just because you are starting out, or unknown, it doesn't mean your words have less value.

Maybe you will be fortunate enough to enter a collaborative partnership? I co-wrote scripts with Robin Stevens, a BAFTA winning writer for children's television, who was generous with his time and knowledge.

Stuff to try

- Connect with writers online via their social media presence. Reply to any posts that interest you. Ask questions at author events.

- Read *'Question & Answer'* sections on author websites. Many will include useful tips, drawn from life experiences.

- Choose a writer and jot down five reasons why you think you would get along (or not).

'I have never experienced another human being. I have experienced my impressions of them.' - Robert Wilson

Write across Genres

Genres are expressed through a multitude of media. Poetry may be presented via the printed word. Stage plays via speech. Portraits utilise the graphic arts.

It is easy to get caught up in one genre, so I purposely write in multiple genres, finding that one often informs another. For instance, picture book stories have a lot in common with radio scripts as each use visual imagery; one via the page and the other through the listeners' imagination.

I use this visual connection to my advantage and sometimes plot stories visually using sticky notes, while loosely sketching all the key beats of the action.

Some authors achieve success and become well-known via one specific genre, such as crime writing. Regardless of genre, I write to the best of my ability. My work carries my name and reputation with it. I want it to open doors, not close them.

Stuff to try

- Jot down genres. Highlight the ones that most interest you. Identify those genres that are expressed via mixed media.

- Explore a genre you don't much care for. Afterwards, reconsider your response. Do you feel differently now?

'Genres aren't closed boxes. Stuff flows back and forth across the borders all the time.' - Margaret Atwood

When to Write?

Paying bills can be a real headache. On average, a professional writer earns much less than the average salary. A recent U.K. survey suggested only 14% or so of authors have writing as their sole income source.

Many have day jobs to supplement their income. The demands of the real world will often get in the way of writing, so it makes sense to listen to your body. To make the most of your time, pinpoint when you are most productive.

Are you a night owl who writes best in the wee small hours? Or an early bird?

Create a schedule by filling the calendar on a mobile phone with upcoming appointments and family commitments. The remaining spaces indicate potential times for writing, and should help with creating a lasting routine.

I occasionally pull an all-nighter to get a project done. This is not sustainable, as I never feel like writing the next day. I try not to be too hard on myself as writing is a rollercoaster, full of ups and downs.

Write when you can.

Stuff to try

- Log each time you write, the duration of each session, and how you feel. Energetic? Tired? Do this for a few weeks then create a schedule to suit.

- Leave pens around the house. Pick one up the moment you feel like writing.

- Give the key people in your life a unique ringtone so you can judge if you need to stop writing to answer a call.

- Incorporate interruptions into your writing. Have a phone ring, a dog bark or a volcano erupt! Make the interruption change the direction of your narrative. Surprise yourself!

- Try writing at the same time each day.

- Curb distractions by switching off your phone, or by playing wordless background music.

- Study the week ahead and pinpoint any likely interruptions. See if you can work around them.

'I write when I'm inspired, and I see to it that I'm inspired at 9 a.m. every morning.' - Peter DeVries

How to Stay Fresh

To keep my writing fresh, I aim to have two stories going at the same time. While writing one, I take a break from the other and revisit it later. I won't work on stories too similar in style or narrative as this can become hard to manage, or confusing.

One way to stay fresh is to write little and often. Use a Pomodoro 'countdown timer' app that rings after a set time on a smartwatch or mobile phone. This sets the pace for a writing session.

I write in short bursts and take regular five or ten minute breaks to disengage from the pressure of writing. I might listen to some music or fuss the dog. Interesting ideas usually bubble up on my return.

Stuff to try

- Pause your latest story and challenge yourself to write the last line or the final paragraph.

- Devise titles for new stories based on objects you see around you.

- Reflect on the last line of your draft story. Now write the first line.

- Read a story and write a counterpoint argument from the opposite perspective.

'When we engage in what we are naturally suited to do, our work takes on the quality of play and it is play that stimulates creativity.' - Linda Naiman

Avoiding Distractions

Install focus boosting software to clear unwanted visual clutter from your computer and prevent the opening of social media content.

The main benefit of such software is its awesome ability to lock down distracting apps, thereby reducing any temptation to pause writing and browse online.

If distractions persist, try to regain control of your thoughts. Picture yourself inside a giant, clear bubble & let the distractions bounce off. Or imaginatively shoot them into the sky and watch them explode like fireworks.

I have a habit of over-editing while I write a first draft, which affects my creative flow. Too much stopping, starting and rearranging can be very distracting so I aim to write in longer chunks, straight through. That way, I don't constantly interrupt myself. Write at least one chapter before going back to fiddle with stuff.

Stuff to try

- Pick a realistic word count. Start writing. Do you work better with a set word count or a set time?

- Stimulate your writing by going for a walk. Be mindful of the environment you pass through. Check out the sights, sounds and smells.

- Write a story in just 50 words. Allow 5 minutes.

'You can always find a distraction if you're looking for one.'

- Tom Kite

Stuff About Stories

What is a Story?

Good question.

A story comprises of a sequence of plotted events, not always in chronological order. Each event links to the next event, as when a thief runs down a corridor, opens a door and sees a safe.

Earlier events can cause later events. A thief opens a door and activates a silent alarm which alerts armed security guards, who then rush in dramatically while the safe is being opened.

Events are either natural or supernatural incidents that create problems. A supernatural event appears to defy laws of nature and rational scientific explanation, though sometimes it has a more down-to earth reason.

As problems escalate so should the tension. Build stories to a believable climax and a satisfying resolution that sums up how a problem was solved.

As a general rule, make sure you know what is taking place in your story. It is fine to keep your readers in the dark about various goings on, but not yourself. If you are hesitant and uncertain about elements within your story it WILL show.

Readers are likely to be put off or become confused and bored.

Stuff to try

- Immerse yourself in different genres, such as science fiction or crime. Identify the main thrust of each story. Is it about new relationships, personal transformation, finding peace, etc? Tease out the general theme.

- Take a story and note the key events at each stage of the plot that drive the narrative, such as the act of saving a person from drowning, or seeing a curtain close.

- Take a simple linear action. (Getting out of bed.) Add more action to it. (Getting out of bed and finding someone underneath.) Then more. Build the scene and the tension.

- Recall confusing stories where you literally lost the plot. Was it because the writer had withheld vital information, or because the story was overloaded with muddled content?

- Summarise a favourite story in one paragraph. Identify the action beats that make up this story.

'Stories of imagination tend to upset those without one.'
- Terry Pratchett

Story Premise and Theme

All stories need a theme. It is what your story will explore. It arises out of an initial premise; the idea behind the story.

In the movie *Spiderman*, you could say the premise is that a man is bitten by a radioactive spider and discovers he has superpowers. So the theme could be 'incredible transformation'. Your theme ought to give your story a relevance and purpose. It should loosely sum up what the story is about.

The theme of *Beauty and the Beast* could easily be 'opposites attract'. I find it useful to distil each story down to a succinct phrase or sentence. A statement that beats with the heart of the narrative.

Be clear in your mind why you are telling a particular story. It will give the plot more focus and your readers greater satisfaction.

Stuff to try

- Devise themes from favourite movies. Compare them to the official movie poster taglines.

- Create a short story using one of these themes - lost & found, seeing red, troubling thoughts, never alone.

'The ideal way to work on a project is to ask a question you don't know the answer to.' - Francis Ford Coppola

Story Arcs

A theme incorporates the main message (or messages) an audience will take away with them.

Television writers like to spread a theme over a story arc that will run across several episodes. The theme is developed and resolved by the way characters overcome conflicts in the story. Emotionally charged story arcs closely relate to the fortunes of characters in the narrative.

The writer's aim is to engage viewers until the end, unfolding layers of conflict, tension and drama. So if the theme is 'invasion', ensure the story arc leads, say, to a suitably dramatic alien landing, and go on to explore good or bad consequences for life on Earth.

Stuff to try

- Map out a series of episodic events about 'loss'.

- Explore a favourite TV drama box set and pull out its key theme(s) and main story arc.

- Take a theme, such as 'unexpected memories' and write a personal response.

'A story has its purpose and its path. It must be told correctly for it to be understood.' - Marcus Sedgwick

Story Titles

Coming up with a memorable title is not always easy. If you already have one before you begin writing it should keep you on theme as you write. Feel free to change the title in light of what you have written.

I usually pull out a phrase that encapsulates the thrust of the story. *The Finders* was one such example. It was a published play for teenage readers about an alien race seeking out lost relatives. And a teenager finding himself.

Some titles convey mystery, such as *From Here to Eternity.* Great titles sell the story ... and the book. They can come from characters, character descriptions, the setting, theme and plot. Or your friends and family. From absolutely anywhere.

It is up to you, and your eventual editor, to decide on which title works best. Then the marketing and sales teams will have an input.

I have been over-ruled once by a publisher and that particular chapter book had fewer sales than the rest in the series.

Stuff to try

- Compile a list of location based titles, e.g., *The Crow Road*.

- List character titles, such as *Goldfinger*.

- Create awful clichéd titles for your stories, and then rework them.

'I usually have no title until the editor has to present the book and calls me frantically.' - Judy Blume

Story Focus

Book titles often suggest the direction a story is going in. I link titles to the main thematic thrust of my stories.

The title of my radio play, *Stranger in the Home*, toys with the unsettling notion of an invasion of privacy. It also alludes to being in a care home for the elderly. I prefer titles that work at more than one level.

Alliteration works well, especially when writing for children. In my picture book, *Beanpole Billy*, I tell the tale of a tall boy who is mistaken for the new class teacher. Titles like this give writers and readers a point of focus. Though, if I'm really honest, I would nowadays steer clear of something that might be construed as 'name calling'.

- Consider why the title *His Dark Materials* works at several levels.

- Explore the possibilities of punning titles and those that share several meanings.

- Come up with the most general title you can about your story. The most abstract. Then the most specific. Which works best for you?

'Titles are not only important, they are essential for me. I cannot write without a title.' - Guillermo Cabrera Infante

Story Development

Newly born stories are similar to babies, because they require considerable nurturing and attention. The potential for greatness is there, but so is the likelihood of an unexpected - nose wrinkling - surprise. New stories have needs.

They demand three-dimensional characters, captivating settings, dynamic plots, robust structures and an engaging style. A lot to consider.

An effective approach is to act on what you are good at. If your forté is character creation, start with that. Work from a position of strength. The whole point of writing is to get ideas out of one's head and onto the page.

And always finish what you have begun.

Stuff to try

- Analyse the strengths in your current story. Do they revolve around solid characters, great dialogue, descriptive prose?

- Explore whether your characters are sufficiently different to each other. Do you fulfil their needs and hopes? Are they conflicted enough to go on a journey?

- Create a main character and ask what they crave. Give this character an obstacle in the way, then devise and write possible solutions.

'The universe is made of stories, not atoms.'
- Muriel Rukeyser

Story Action

A story is a journey. Think about it for a moment. Every story is a journey.

One that progresses through a series of actions. Readers want to read about characters doing things or having things done to them.

A book about someone reading on the deck of a ship is way more interesting when that ship is the Titanic, ploughing headlong into an iceberg!

When writing static scenes, swaddle them within a dynamic, bigger picture. Conversely, dynamic scenes benefit from moments of calm. Let the action unfold at an appropriate pace to drive the narrative forward.

Stuff to try

- Consider the step by step actions required to make a cup of tea. Go into as much detail as you can.

- Describe the final moments of the Titanic purely through action. Now cut out as much descriptive text as you dare.

- Action often arises from the emotional needs of characters. Someone does something for some reason. Or, at first glance, no reason. Have fun identifying the root cause.

'Action expresses priorities.' - Mahatma Gandhi

'I think it's my adventure, my trip, my journey, and I guess my attitude is, let the chips fall where they may.'
- Leonard Nimoy

Story Reaction

Stories need consequences. These come from plot actions and character reactions. Most stories revolve around the actions of key characters, who must live with (and react physically and emotionally to) the knock-on effects of their actions.

Story conveys emotion. Plot conveys action. Stories are created when plotted action unfolds. Thus when the dog dies, the owner cries. The story progresses via cause and effect. Out of *this* comes *that*.

Stuff to try

- Stories are about what a character wants *and* what stops them from getting it. Think up examples.

- Identify action beats in a plot. Are they all helping to tell the story? Pinpoint any consequences.

- Do the same for one of your stories. Identify and remove any actions that slow the story down.

'Writing a story or a novel is one way of discovering sequence in experience, of stumbling upon cause and effect in the happenings of a writer's own life.'
- Eudora Welty

Story Consequences

Good or bad decisions creates consequences, and consequences are essential if a story is to have meaning.

Characters must care at some level about the consequences of their actions, or other people's actions. I like to show characters having internal dialogues at odds with their outward actions. This creates tension.

An introverted character may struggle with winning a million pounds, and feel under pressure, not wanting the responsibility. How would you feel?

Stuff to try

- Create a character with zero morals and no regard for consequences. Play with the result.

- Start with 'She opens the box' and write a sequence of ever more deadly consequences.

- Imperil a character under a deflating hot air balloon. Consider their options, pick one, and explore its consequences.

'A man does what he must in spite of personal consequences, in spite of obstacles and dangers and pressures and that is the basis of all human morality.'
- Winston Churchill

Deeper Stuff

Conflict

Stories need conflict, internal or external. Characters can be in conflict with themselves or other characters.

One of my published stories involves a boy being mistaken for the teacher on his first day. Immediately conflicted by what to do, he chooses to teach the class - with comic consequences.

Characters can also be pitted in conflict against external forces.

Any conflict must be believably resolved, not sorted by an outside god-like agency.

Be wary of using coincidence, or blind chance, to resolve issues. Readers feel cheated when a character is let off too easily.

Stuff to try

- Study stories that feature similar types of conflict, e.g., alien invasion stories like *War of the Worlds* and *Day of the Triffids*.

- Conflict isn't always bad. Come up with situations where this is true. Where is the line crossed?

- Examine the ways conflict can be resolved; persuading, haggling, negotiating, yielding, capitulating.

- Identify particular adversaries. Popular ones might be animals, machines, fate, society, or destructive elements from the natural or supernatural world.

'The harder the conflict, the more glorious the triumph.'

- Thomas Paine

Problem to Fix

Every interesting story has a problem to fix that usually arises out of conflict.

It is a dramatic problem that affects the characters so much their only option is to tackle it head on. Inaction is never a good solution. The interest lies in if, when and how the storyteller's characters succeed or fail. Life-saving or life-threatening situations offer up interesting problems. So do smaller scale conflicts, such as sibling rivalry or neighbourhood disputes.

Put metaphorical bumps in the road that characters must avoid. Their journey should not go too smoothly.

Stuff to try

- List the problems you have encountered in the past year, big or small. Do any inspire a story?

- Scour newspapers for interesting stories involving problems that have either been solved or are ongoing. What type are you most drawn to?

- Peruse a magazine's problem page and create new characters to explore any conflicts that are being aired.

'We can't solve problems by using the same kind of thinking we used when we created them.' - Albert Einstein

Emotional Connections

A story stimulates when it arouses emotions and feelings in the reader, while also creating empathy with characters and plot.

Well-written emotional dramatic arcs have the power to stimulate oxytocin production in readers, keeping them neurologically engaged as their senses interact with newly created imagined worlds.

Truly engaging stories incorporate tipping points, where the action veers off in unexpected directions. A sudden unexpected detour will raise questions, create surprise and subvert expectations.

Build suspense by holding things back. Let readers experience events as they unfold. Drip-feed details and leave everyone wanting more. I like to begin a story with a big event. Hit the ground running and let readers catch up!

Stuff to try

- Create opening lines on the theme of 'revenge'.

- Think of a negative situation. What single event, remark or action might tip someone over the edge?

- Write about an emotional event without saying what it is.

'Writers and painters alike are in the business of consulting their own imaginations, and stimulating the imaginations of others.'- Lynne Truss

Four Story Types

Writers have an infinite number of stories available to them. Ones with monsters, quests, superheroes, troubled souls, abductions, transformations, disasters, underdogs, rivalry, revenge, deliverance, love or maybe a rite of passage.

It helps to know what type of story you want to write. I am drawn to these four story types.

Born Again stories; where a character undergoes an internal - often gradual - transformation and acts differently afterwards. [*A Christmas Carol* by Dickens]

Disruption stories; where a disrupted world is put right (or improved for the better) by the courageous heroism of the characters, usually the lead one. [*Harry Potter* books by J.K. Rowling]

Journey stories; where characters physically or mentally enter a new world, adapt to it, and return. Not always triumphant, but maybe wiser. Perhaps involves a quest, or overcoming something bigger than they are. [*The Hobbit* by Tolkien]

Question stories; where at least one mystery is presented and - after various false trails - is solved. Perhaps by a detective, a private investigator or a hapless bystander sucked into the conspiratorial goings on. [Anything by the celebrated mystery writer Agatha Christie.] Invariably, there is an overlap between these four basic story models.

Stuff to try

- Born Again stories. Look for the obvious similarities within them. Who or what is reborn? How and why? Reflect on the attraction of this particular type of story. Is it redemption? Having a second chance?

- Rags to Riches is a Journey story. A character starts off with nothing and ends up with everything. It could also be a Born Again story, a Question or Disruption story. Do you agree?

- Identify the kind of stories that you most prefer to read. Is this reflected in your writing?

- Seek out other story models.

'Time is a sort of river of passing events, and strong is its current.' - Marcus Aurelius

Born Again Story

These are character-driven narratives where the protagonist is transformed in some way over the course of the story. An obvious example is Scrooge in *A Christmas Carol* by Charles Dickens. When you imbue a character with an emotional, physical or spiritual transformation, your words gain greater significance, especially when they touch on transformative changes in your readers' lives. Only when characters are aware of a change will they reap the fruits of it. Enlightenment is a key theme in such stories. Not all born again stories have happy endings.

Stuff to try

- Consider how you use descriptive text to describe transformative change.

- Select characters from one of your stories. Consider how they could change and be transformed in a positive or negative way.

- Take a character from a troubled state to being at peace through a series of challenges. Go on a twisting route with setbacks and breakthroughs.

'Knowing others is wisdom, knowing yourself is Enlightenment.' - Lao Tzu

Disruption Story

Disruption stories start with an event that changes the previous way of living (or looking at things).

They might involve an asteroid strike or a win on the lottery. Perhaps a character losing their memory.

The narrative would seek to create some kind of normality for the characters. A New World Order.

Maybe the narrative begins a moment after the disruptive event, which is revealed slowly via flashback over later chapters?

These stories work when the changed world is believable and invokes tension. In *The Children of Men* by P D James, no children are being born and it appears civilisation will die out because of an infertility defect in the population. Who will survive?

Stuff to try

- Make a list of life-disrupting events according to their magnitude and knock-on effects. See if there are any you wish to write about. How much control did you have?

- Disruption stories begin with a major event that causes other events to unfold. Explore what that major event might be. Exploding volcanoes and planes provide a dramatic impetus for action stories.

- Write a disruption story titled *Hope*.

- The disruption can also be more personal, such as a divorce. Think back over your life to moments where things changed direction. Did you meet someone unexpectedly? Were you facing health issues?

'The conscious purpose of science is control of Nature; its unconscious effect is disruption and chaos.'
- William Irwin Thompson

Journey Story

Journey stories involve a character who physically or mentally enters a new world, then adapts and returns. It can be a literal new world, as in landing on Mars, or a fanciful one, such as Alice tumbling into Wonderland.

A Journey story allows the reader to discover all about a world *at the same time as* the character. Reader and protagonist share the same view, but may react differently to what each sees.

There is no need to describe the world before your character sees it. Let it unfold alongside the narrative. This unfolding of the unknown will help build tension. It is especially effective in detective stories.

Stuff to try

- Characters may go on internal journeys while participating on a quest. Something changes them on the way. Identify stories where this occurs. Are they more satisfying?

- Unfamiliar worlds offer characters unfamiliar challenges. Frodo, in *Lord of the Rings* by Tolkien, has to adapt to survive. Find other examples.

- Journeys can take place in a localised area. Play with limiting the geography of the world. Limit your character to exploring a recently discovered attic room.

'There are no foreign lands. It is the traveller only who is foreign.' - Robert Louis Stevenson

Question Story

Question stories (often crime-based *whodunits*) pose questions for characters, who must follow events in the hope of gathering knowledge and answers.

It is usual practice to place a question at the start of a crime narrative to hook the reader's interest. Then end with a clear solution that resolves the mystery.

The question must be big enough to sustain the narrative. This is why murders feature highly in crime fiction. My partner, an avid crime fiction reader, says the best examples in the genre avoid coincidences, accidental reveals and unconvincing dialogue.

Some stories conclude with a supplementary question. This only works if the initial question in the story has been resolved. Otherwise readers won't care.

Stuff to try

- Reflect on the questions raised in stories that you have read. Were they big enough? Satisfying? Worth answering? Look out for obvious plotting or weak characterisation.

- Detectives often share traits with the villain they seek. This adds complexity to the drama. Consider how these shared traits enhance the writing.

'Don't become a mere recorder of facts, but try to penetrate the mystery of their origin.' - Ivan Pavlov

Generating Narratives

I use a single sentence framework for creating, or simply describing, a story.

> My story is about (person) who (obstacle) but (solution).

Here is an example, taken from a story I wrote for young readers.

> Amy's Armbands is about a girl who is afraid of water but discovers she can swim in the sky instead.

I try to sum up the story's theme too.

> The theme of Amy's Armbands is 'overcoming fear'.

That's it. Pretty simple.

Stuff to try

- Create three single line plot summaries using this format.

- Now play with incorporating multiple obstacles.

- Assign a theme to each of your simple summaries.

'When you do enough research, the story almost writes itself. Lines of development spring loose and you'll have choices galore.' - Robert McKee

Creating Characters

Character characteristics

Stories are driven forward by the main plot or the main character. Plot-based narratives crack on at a pace, while character pieces can afford to dwell on details.

Some books pull off both.

Though arguably a convincing character, such as detective John Rebus in Ian Rankin's crime novels, is secondary to the murderous plotting which must sustain the journey.

A character's personality is indicated by emotional reactions to external stimuli, or the actions and reactions from other people.

Each character requires a clear point of view. This arises from a believably engaging and enticing backstory.

Rather than creating characters in isolation, I always consider their internal and external relationships to each other.

Minor characters need something to do. Let them challenge and confront the beliefs and actions of main characters.

The big question I ask is ...

What role must each character fulfil to tell a good story?

Stuff to try

- Characters are more interesting when they desire things. Create two opposing characters with conflicting desires.

- To up the interest, also give them similar traits.

- Adversity can shape personality. Identify problems your characters must confront. Give these characters personal qualities to almost, but not quite, deal with them.

- A character ought to have inherent weaknesses as well as strengths. This makes the journey to a desired goal more challenging. Consider the types of strengths and weaknesses that characters in your latest story possess. Use only those traits that push your story forward.

- When a minor character confronts a main character, consider how this interaction could alter a protagonist's state of mind, or change the direction and course of a story.

"When writing a novel a writer should create living people; people not characters. A character is a caricature." - Ernest Hemingway, Death in the Afternoon

Stereotypes

Stereotypical characters are shallow and possess generalised character traits. They have no deep purpose or ability to deal with change.

Meaningful characters are more realistic, with evolving personalities and an inner drive. Their dialogue will always be more convincing.

It may be tempting to define characters via exaggerated or oversimplified stereotypes, e.g., a heroic firefighter or a brave police officer.

To get a better sense of personality, go past obvious traits and identify hidden characteristics. Firefighters may have doubts, health problems and emotional trauma to deal with. Police officers may be worn out or fearful.

On a side note, archetypes tend to be general examples, broader concepts of a particular idea such as the hero or the lover, as typified by Ancient Greek gods.

Make characters more engaging by giving them a memorable characteristic or two.

Add props to provide an easy-to-read clue to a character's personality. Use them to play against type. Peter Sellers (Inspector Clouseau) in the *Trail of the Pink Panther* movies gestures with a pipe to seem sophisticated but almost burns down his office.

Consider adding a movement, a mannerism or a look. A limp, a nervous head scratch or even a coat of colourful tartan fur!

Describe the appearance of each character in a couple of specific sentences or paragraphs. Just enough to let readers gain a clear visual impression.

Stuff to try

- The detective Sherlock Holmes has his pipe and deerstalker hat, plus pithy dialogue that reflects his quick wits. Identify your personal characteristics and ask a few people you know to highlight more. Are there any you didn't know you had? I tried this and discovered I sort of, basically, say sort of and basically a lot.

- Describe a casually dressed person with a few sketchy sentences. Add a few more details, such as a crumpled shirt and scuffed shoes.

- Now describe in depth a formally dressed character. Get them both to talk to each other.

- Jot down a list of characters from books. Note their key characteristics. Is it a prop like

Mary Poppins' umbrella? Or is it the way your characters walk, talk and gesture?

'If he's a powerful character, unless you give him vulnerability, I don't think he'll be as interesting to the reader.' - Stan Lee

Character names

In *Mixed-Up Myths*, a reworking of two Greek tales, I had fun with names.

My first tale - *The Mint Choc Touch* - involved a girl called Rukma who magically turns anything she touches into ice cream. Rukma can be translated as Golden. A nod to magical King Midas who had the power to turn things into gold.

Young readers love puns. I chose the name Rex for a character who wrecks things. I avoid trendy children's names completely as they quickly date.

Some names are too closely linked to well-known individuals or popular imaginary characters. [Adele, Taylor, Harry, Buffy, Bart] So, unless I am making a deliberate reference, I steer clear.

Names should fit characters. Tony does not really cut it for a menacing space alien. Likewise, Ethelred is not a name you will readily hear in the local park.

Sometimes authors play against type. Sue Hendra, who writes popular picture books for young readers, gives her funny characters names like Barry, Keith and

Norman. The comedy comes from the ordinariness. It is a bit like naming your cat Steve.

When writing for children, choose authentic character names that are easy to say yet memorable. Many of the names in my stories have just one or two syllables. Short and punchy. To avoid confusion, I tend not to give characters in a story any names that begin with the same initial letter.

Stuff to try

- To add extra depth to your characters, browse through a baby name book, where the origins and meanings are provided.

- Collate nicknames, abbreviations and affectionate terms to make your writing more realistic. Put two unusual names together, such as Lemony Snicket.

- Pair the start of one name with the end of another to create unusual portmanteau names. Jessica and Emily could become Jemily!

- Come up with a nickname for all of your characters, based on each one's backstory.

'If names are not correct, language will not be in accordance with the truth of things.' - Confucius

Settings

In the mood

Characters have to exist somewhere. A place that lets their story unfold. The best settings evoke a sensory response from the reader.

Places evoke moods. I once hurried away from an eerie building on the east coast of Scotland that was shaped like a giant pineapple! I knew I had made the right decision when a murder of crows shattered the silence as they scattered skyward.

Let your setting act like an extra character. Picture a lost polar explorer, trudging across a vast unforgiving snow-blasted wasteland, pitted against the elements. Fear, hope, despair could all come into play.

The setting often influences a character's mood, as when someone is approaching a supposedly haunted castle, or entering a narrow, dark smugglers' tunnel.

Conflicts arise when settings appear to turn against characters. The story becomes more interesting as we try to work out how the character might respond to, say, a swirling tornado or an approaching mist.

Characters come to life when they react to a setting. Let them gasp at the touch of hot sand between their toes or the sudden cold splash of an unexpected wave. When describing reactions, less is more.

Stuff to try

- Evoke a bustling scene by varying the length of sentences. Use short staccato sentences when describing fleeting views from a speeding train, or longer sentences when describing weary characters trudging up a steep slope.

- Whenever a character needs to register a scene slowly, make your writing match this and eke out emerging details. Place characters in an unfamiliar environment and explore their reaction.

- Write with brevity and focus whenever a character is bombarded with the sights, sounds and smells of a dynamic scene. Choose a shocking moment to explore.

'We have little power to choose what happens, but ... complete power over how we respond.' - A. Huffington

Static or Dynamic

Settings change just like a person's mood. A swirl of wind casually causing fallen petals to dance, an ice-flecked avalanche thundering ever closer, a courtroom echoing to the yells of angry onlookers. The world around us affects our thoughts and external actions.

While some setting changes are dramatic, others are less noticeable but still elicit a dramatic reaction; as when a tiny, repetitive flicker from a lightbulb in a prison cell tips a character into insanity.

Time plays its part too. In *Great Expectations* by Charles Dickens, Pip observes decrepit Miss Havisham in her dilapidated mansion:

"I saw that the bride within the bridal dress had withered like the dress, and like the flowers, and had no brightness left but the brightness of her sunken eyes."

Stuff to try

- Describe settings using similes, e.g., 'The weary train commuters were crammed together like broken biscuits in a tin.'

- Put a group of confident and introvert characters in an abandoned house. Describe their emotional state(s) as they walk around. Vary sentence length to match their individual moods.

- Visualise your settings as characters with moods. It is easy to imagine an angry or calm sea, but what about a desert or an office?

'One does not love a place the less because one has suffered in it.' - Virginia Woolf

Real or Imagined

One of the benefits of using a real setting is the opportunity to physically explore it. Evoked emotions can be channelled to guide what a character might be thinking.

When writing about a particular physical place in the world, it makes sense to add convincing descriptions because your reader may have been there too. That's when detailed research comes in.

I used an online search engine to gather images and facts about Loch Ness for one particular story set in that area. I also drew on memories of a recent trip there. Having physically experienced the setting, it was easier for me to put it into words. I could draw on all my sense to create a sense of place.

It helps to be sparing with facts. One well-known author who had a dramatic bestselling book about Leonardo da Vinci has a habit of pausing the action to drone on at length about a location's history or geographical significance. This level of detail kills the pace and stunts the reader's interest.

Imagined places require a certain level of realism to allow the reader to connect. They also need the equivalent of a character's backstory. The shadowy house in the movie *Psycho* plays a huge part in creating suspense, with danger lurking around every corner.

One last point. A teacher will be more familiar in a classroom than a detective who is there to arrest a pupil, so play with a character's level of interaction. Explore how characters register an environment differently.

Stuff to try

- Overlong descriptions of buildings and environments will slow or kill the pace of a story. So keep things moving and drip-feed the setting into the action. 'He ran lightly across the gravel path.' Less is more.

- Choose a location and research its history. Look for something that will trigger a story. In Glasgow, I spotted a 19th century stone wall carving of cherubs and one appeared to be reading an iPad!

- Put one of your characters in the location, having arrived unexpectedly. Write what happens next.

- Devise a dynamic setting that alters over the story, perhaps with changing seasons. Use big brushstrokes to develop a sense of place, then add finer details for key elements.

- Create a story in one setting. Maybe a locked room mystery? Let the limitations of space liberate you.

'Are you really sure a floor can't also be a ceiling?' - Escher

Stuff about Plots

Plot and Structure

Plot and Structure are not the same thing.

The plot is a sequence of connected events. The stuff that actually happens in a story. It exists to make actions meaningful.

Plots are free to meander all over the place as characters react and do stuff. Cause and effect.

Structure is how you tell your story. Where you place chunks of narrative for the best emotional impact. I see it as the trellis around which the plot weaves.

When I wrote about a heroic car called Brum, for a popular BBC children's TV show, I followed a set structure:

Establisher [of setting and characters]
Trigger Incident [such as theft]
Chase [of thieves]
Rescue [of stolen goods]
Resolution [all back as it was]

Various plots within this structure involved baddies stealing money, paintings, even a garden gnome. As young viewers watched a plotted sequence of action-packed events, they became familiar with the structure, and looked forward to seeing how each episode's plot played out. That was a simple example. More often there will be a main plot based around the central character, and a supporting subplot or two.

A funny plot needs light and shade. Moments where the joking slows or stops. I am reminded of old black and white movies where slapstick humour unfolds at a frenetic pace. This relentlessness soon ceases to be amusing. That is why subplots are so useful.

Providing a much needed change, a subplot is like a refreshing intermezzo sorbet that cleanses the palate. A good subplot exists to support and strengthen the main plot.

- Pick a novel that was turned into a television show. Go through both formats, identifying the underlying structure of each.

- Now identify any obvious structural changes. What has been added/left out? Consider why.

- Read a fiction book and check out the blurb on the back cover. How much of the plot was revealed? Where did the blurb stop short? Explore what was left out and why.

'Character is plot, plot is character.' - F. Scott Fitzgerald

Drama and Plot

Plots elicit emotional responses. From characters and us. Charged moments that spark a sequence of events. A mysterious explosion may be the result of one character's angry scheming or another's despondency with life.

Drama comes from readers caring about characters. If characters are deliberately unemotional, we must engage with the emotions they generate in other characters, or in us. Conflicted characters must be forced into action; taken to a turning point where their life situations change [for good or bad]. Without emotion there can be no drama.

Dramatic conflicts occur in all relationships, both personal and business. It might be as simple as a frustrated parent dealing with a grumpy toddler [Been there], or a stressed writer blaming management failings and quitting in front of the boss [Done that].

Stuff to try

- Take a story in any format and seek out the points of high drama. Identify any accompanying emotional peaks and troughs of the characters.

- Choose a highly dramatic and extremely antagonistic moment and swap the emotions over, so anger becomes sadness. Explore how this swap alters the narrative.

'Drama is life with the dull bits cut out.' - Alfred Hitchcock

Subplots

A protagonist railing against a persistent antagonist is quite interesting to observe, but the emotional content ratchets up a notch when someone else is involved; often a person the main character confides in.

This added dimension is where subplots develop and secondary layers of complexity are introduced. A subplot takes a reader away from the main plot. How much, depends on you.

Each subplot will have its own narrative journey, but must not feel too disconnected. Subplots should feed into the main theme *and* have a recognisable beginning, middle and end.

So if 'discovering truth' is your overall theme and the main plot is about an autistic child trying to solve a mystery as to who murdered a dog, then a subplot about finding what happened to the boy's absent mother will strengthen the whole story.

As it does in *The Curious Incident of the Dog in the Night-Time* by Mark Haddon.

I tend to keep things simple when writing for young readers. One main plot and a subplot. I do this mainly because my focus is usually on the wordplay and comic action.

When I write a subplot, I need it to converge with the main plot at a convenient future point. In one of my chapter books, a character called Isla becomes invisible. She is able to use her invisibility to help Porridge the Tartan Cat win the Best Pet trophy and beat his nemesis, a pesky poodle.

Subplot / main plot interlinking should take place whether you write for children or adults. It provides cohesion, and binds the reader closer to the narrative.

Obviously, there can be more than one subplot when writing longer novels. You may have one subplot aligned with the main theme and a second railing against it.

Stuff to try

- Subplots help the main plot along, often indirectly. Weave a subplot into your story so its outcome helps the main character out of a tricky situation (and go on to succeed).

- A subplot may arise when the values of characters clash. Create two very different characters and weigh up their values. Find a trigger point where their views clash and explore it.

'I have a plan, one I've been plotting for years now. It is my only way out' - John Grisham

Subplots and Exposition

Movies revel in subplots. One of the best examples is a subplot in Jurassic Park where an IT engineer steals dinosaur DNA but meets a sticky end, which means the IT systems cannot be turned back on. His nefarious actions trigger huge consequences, namely a dinosaur rampage.

Occasionally a subplot is there purely to explain why an event happened. It must be used sparingly because giving readers a chunk of expositional information, typically via a narrator or a particular character, interrupts the flow of the story and could become tedious.

Exposition has its uses, as seen in traditional fairy tales. 'Once upon a time there was a little girl called Goldilocks who went for a walk, feeling hungry.' Also in comic book stories, such as an explanation of how a hero got superpowers.

I tend to avoid exposition and may instead write a flashback to an earlier event, so the reader is present as the action unfolds. This gives each reader a chance to interpret the scene and make up their own mind as to what took place.

A tightly plotted story that tells things visually is less likely to rely on unwanted information dumping.

Stuff to try

- Find an example of exposition in your writing. Rework the information to be more entertaining, perhaps in flashback or flashforward format.

- Have fun spotting terrible scenes of dull exposition in your favourite books or movies.

- Snippets of exposition, in the form of justifying or explaining past events, can be slipped into the dialogue when two or more characters converse with each other. Have a go at writing this way.

'Don't judge each day by the harvest you reap, but by the seeds you plant.' - Robert Louis Stevenson

Stuff about Twists

Twisting Plots

Playwright William Shakespeare used complicated plots called imbroglios; deliberating confusing the audience with identical twins, mistaken identities, etc.

Being no great shakes, I keep things simple when I write for children. When I write for adults, I also keep things simple.

Emotional impact is lost when readers struggle to keep up with the plot. Have just enough plot to satisfy your readers. Of course, still bend it around a bit. Add a twist or two.

Plot twists should surprise, entertain, provoke, satisfy and make sense!

In *Rebecca*, by Daphne Du Maurier, Maxim de Winter still worships his deceased first wife Rebecca, despite marrying for a second time. Her bedroom is a shrine. As the story develops, Rebecca's apparently perfect past comes under scrutiny, and readers are forced to re-evaluate what they know.

Stuff to try

- Plot a simple sequence of events. Drop in a twist that will affect one of your characters in a good way, while giving another problems.

'When ... some event suddenly seemed to illuminate things that had gone before, I was as surprised as anyone else.' - Douglas Adams

Shocking Twists

Some plot twists have a strong shock value. Characters may discover they are not who they think they are, or the world they inhabit is not actually real.

In my futuristic playscript, *Another Level*, a child playing a computer game turns out to be living unwittingly in a computer game. The twist being that his world fades to black when the game is switched off. It was a new idea at the time, as was virtual reality technology.

Twists do not have to be at the end of a story. Writers use them to send plots in unexpected directions. They may have a sudden impact or a slow build.

Before I Go to Sleep by S.J. Watson has a brilliant premise. Christine, an amnesiac, wakes each morning unable to remember where she is. Or the nature of her relationship with her husband, Ben. She writes a daily journal, but that serves only to deepen the mystery. One day she reads a self-penned warning not to trust Ben. Slowly, as more layers are peeled off, her suspicion grows.

Stuff to try

- Find plots that have great shock endings. Consider ones that work well visually. Study the set up and pay off.

- Investigate how misdirection played a part.

'Every story ever told can be broken down into three parts. The beginning. The middle. And the plot twist.'
- R.L. Stine

Revelatory Twists

A common plot twist found in crime novels is the red herring, where suspicion falls on a particular individual but is misplaced, because it subsequently turns out that someone else did it. Crime writers Agatha Christie and Conan Doyle often laid puzzling trails of false and misleading clues.

A kindred twist may occur when a character suddenly has the realisation that what they believe is true about themselves is actually false. (A child who believes she is an orphan suddenly discovers her family are still alive.)

When Neo in the *Matrix* movies discovers his understanding of the real world is completely wrong, this newfound knowledge spurs him into being a heroic force for good against malevolent entities that are controlling the fate of humanity.

The False Protagonist plot device is another interesting way to provide a twist. In Alfred Hitchcock's celebrated horror film, *Psycho*, Marion Crane (played by Janet Leigh) appears to be the main character. Just as we are getting to know her, Norman Bates (Antony Perkins) comes along to provide a memorably shocking shower scene. After this, the focus is on Norman's unsettling story.

Falsehood is also a feature of the False Hero plot device. An audience roots for a particular character, only to discover this person is not what they appear to be. I saw an example of this as a child when I read *The Brave Little Tailor*, from Grimm's Fairy Tales.

The tailor in question is bothered by flies and kills 'seven in one blow'. He inscribes this achievement onto a belt. Later, he has to prove himself against a disbelieving giant. Eventually the resourceful and manipulative tailor marries a princess, but his past comes back to haunt him.

Twists may reveal secrets and falsehoods. They may mislead and misdirect. They may even turn winners into losers (and vice versa). It is no surprise that the best twists contain an element of ... surprise.

Stuff to try

- List as many clichéd plot twists as you can. Consider how you could breathe life into them.

- Someone turns out not to be dead and is the murderer. This scenario features in many crime novels. Put a new spin on this old idea.

- The Butler did it. Explain how, with a twist.

- Find examples of the False Hero. Explore the moment of realisation where a falsehood is revealed. How does the writer convey the revelation to the reader?

'All writers are liars. They twist events to suit themselves. They make use of their own tragedies to make a better story... They are terrible people.' - Nina Bawden

Cliffhangers

Hanging from a cliff is not my idea of fun. But it can make for an exciting moment in a novel.

Victorian author Arthur Conan Doyle's *The Hound of The Baskervilles* came out over nine months in *The Strand* magazine, to great excitement. Doyle was adept at creating cliffhanging endings that put characters in jeopardy. This approach practically guaranteed the next issue would be purchased.

Cliffhangers relate to a moment of peril, danger, shock or mystery. The reader wants to know whether the character will perish, survive, become trapped, escape, etc. How will the character react to adversity or the unknown?

A cliffhanger works best at the end of a chapter, where the solution can be immediately found over the next page. It is easier to build to one moment of high drama at the end of a chapter, than negotiate a lot of small ones.

Cliffhangers often have a shock value. Something unexpected takes place and the character has to react to it. It might simply be the arrival of a person thought to be dead. Or the pilot parachuting out of a plane. The important thing here is that writers leave the readers guessing.

Discovering new information can give rise to a cliffhanging chapter ending. Blood turns out to be tomato sauce!

A character can rack up tension by demanding something happens immediately. Will the command be actioned? What are the consequences if not?

Sometimes characters feel they are really up against it, and helpfully sum up their sorry situation. The bridge is down. There's no way back. If we are invested in the story and rooting for them, we want to see what they do next.

If cliffhangers have a weakness, it is that they may strike a too-similar note. Tension is racked up quickly then released. Too many cliffhangers in one story risk boring or antagonising readers. I am no fan of cliffhangers with clichéd, overlong or irrelevant action.

Stuff to try

- Author Jeffrey Deaver is a modern master of cliffhangers. It is said he aims to put one at the end of every chapter. Read some of his crime novels to explore how he does it.

- Consider why some story cliffhangers are less successful than others.

- Plot a sequence of events leading from a key character's minor mishap to a dramatic cliffhanger moment.

- Enhance the impact by describing a character's emotions before and during the event. Go from a flat emotional state to a highly charged one in a single paragraph.

'The bow too tensely strung is easily broken.' - Publilius

Exploring Your Style

Finding a Voice

Characters must have a voice to express their individuality, even those who do not speak. They require a way of communicating that differentiates them from others.

One character may have a colloquial speaking style which leaves sentences unfinished and words truncated. Another character may use pauses to express hesitation and doubt.

Others could sprinkle sentences with neutral vowel sounds, such as 'um' or 'er'. Fillers that allow them to continue a conversation while they think up something to say.

All these verbal elements enforce the idea that your characters are real, relatable people. Regardless of genre, aim to give each character a unique voice.

I prefer to vary the length and complexity of words that my characters use. While writing a radio play about frustrated teenagers, I incorporated ear-jarring slang words, though with care as I didn't want the story to become too easily dated.

Take a moment to listen to people around you. Notice how they like to use phrases linked to certain senses: 'I hear what you say'. 'I feel for you'. 'I can see what you're getting at'. 'I'm looking for an answer'.

Characters use sensory language to express their emotional state, or to indicate how they engage with the world. Through their visual (seeing), auditory (hearing) or kinaesthetic (feeling & movement) responses.

I use this predilection to tie each character to a particular sense. It is a satisfying way to quickly build, and show off, each character's uniqueness.

Everything I write contains funny elements, even the serious stuff. My radio play - *Kenny* - was about fear and regret, yet it had elements of humour. A reviewer in *The Times* likened the humorous dialogue to the quick-fire old-time Music Hall acts.

My writing style is my calling card. It has to reflect me.

Stuff to try

- Which sense do you refer to most when you communicate with others?

- Stylistically, the writing in my radio plays is very visual, almost filmlike, and creates images for listeners to imagine. I like to keep adjectives and adverbs to a minimum. Too many slow the action down. The less detail I give, the more the audience are able to fill in the gaps. Try this approach.

- Watch online videos or observe people as they go about their business. Focus on the way they speak and generate a useful bank of character voices. Jot down any local phrases you hear on your travels.

'It is not the voice that commands the story, it is the ear.'
- Italo Calvino

Finding Truth

Creative writing requires imagination. Authors invariably draw on their life experiences, knowledge and skills. But what of the time when we wish to write outside our personal world to depict characters from another culture, race or gender?

Crossing the divide from knowing to imagining.

Authors may be in the entertainment business, but we have a responsibility to be truthful.

Clichéd writing does not reflect a culture. It diminishes it. Characters and the lives they lead must be realistic, representative and show people living truthful lives.

To avoid cultural appropriation, where authors fail to write truthfully because they have not been in a position to have lived the truth, I must ask myself some questions. Am I qualified to write in this way? Should I leave it to someone else?

If I am to write in another's voice, I must think how best to depict the lives of my characters in the most respectful, honest and truthful way. My books feature boys and girls. I take care to ensure the children I write about are recognisable

The Finders depicts teenagers at school, and describes how an unexpected change transforms all their lives. Realistic characters required in-depth research. I explored social media, talked with teenagers and identified what interested them, while also reading widely.

I tried to avoid unrepresentative generalisations. Even then, I could only give a snapshot.

Stuff to try

- Read *The Curious Incident of The Dog in the Night Time* where Mark Haddon sensitively explores the life of an autistic boy.

- Research your characters thoroughly to make them individual, and give them truthful hopes, goals and fears.

'No human culture is inaccessible to someone who makes the effort to understand, to learn, to inhabit another world.' - Henry Gates Jr.

Finding Respect

I lived my childhood in the UK Care system. Only when looking back could I see the immense challenges and turbulence involved. I do not see myself as a survivor or victim. I'm not one for labels.

I find it frustrating to read stories where children with Care experience are typically depicted as needy, broken, alone and desperate. Some authors use the orphan trope as a mechanism to get adults out of the way, leaving child characters free to do things unsupervised.

I welcome diligent authors who wish to understand the views and experiences of children in Care, and respect what took place. I am aware I now lead quite a privileged life, so when it comes to writing as someone else, I would not wish my characters to portray a false world, where I misrepresent or stereotype a particular group of people.

Stuff to try

- Read about cultures and lifestyles different to your own. Explore each unique voice and reflect on the urgency, passion and clarity emanating from these lived experiences.

'If we lose love and self-respect for each other, this is how we finally die.' - Maya Angelou

Finding Variety

Your style will vary according to the type of book you write. I write a lot of picture books, and focus on my main character's action and intent. The language is less complex, the story more direct.

I put in just enough text to tell the tale; incorporating onomatopoeia, memorable rhythms and words that are fun to say out loud. I leave creative space for the illustrator to interpret the story.

Dashiell Hammett, author of *The Maltese Falcon*, often used short, punchy sentences.

Gabriel García Márquez, author of *One Hundred Years of Solitude*, chose long, complex - somewhat meandering - sentences, which evoke a sense of time passing slowly.

James Joyce employed a novel stream of consciousness approach.

Maya Angelou wrote with a powerful and lyrical directness that amplified autobiographical experiences of growing up in a segregated, fragmented country.

Stuff to try

- The tone of your writing helps set the style. Are you going for a hard-boiled crime noir approach or an elaborate gothic mystery? Think back to the tone of your latest piece of narrative writing. How well does it marry with the overall theme of your story?

- *'They will never find me in here.'* Use this writing prompt to create two short stories. Vary the sentence length so one is punchier than the other.

- Chris Brookmyre, an author of adult crime fiction, writes acutely observed stories that occasionally veer into anarchy and offer satire with a Scottish twist. Choose three favourite authors and succinctly summarise their styles.

- I usually add elements for adults who may be reading my children's books. In one story, an oven's dial *'goes up to eleven'*, which references a gag from the movie Spinal Tap. Consider your audience and see if you can incorporate additional appealing elements. *'Never, in one place, had he seen so many glum faces.' 'The bridge was intact, just.' 'As the snow in Central Park swirled, I felt like I was alone at the top of the world.'*

- Similes and metaphors have a place in prose as well as poetry. They can add to a persuasive argument by creating unexpected visual juxtapositions and surprising connections. Play with these elements.

'When an author is too meticulous about his style, you may presume that his mind is frivolous and his content flimsy.' - Seneca

Finding the Right Recipe

I like to dip into books to see the styles of other writers. I try to guess each story's theme and pinpoint the flow of the plots.

My tip here is to read every book you can lay your eyes on. Good or bad. Awful writing will not contaminate you, but it will help you develop a feeling for what personally works.

Stuck for a good word or phrase? Then flick through a few chapters and stop at any sentence that appeals to you. Twist it, tweak it. Pull it apart. Use it to stimulate ideas.

Be a book baker.

Create your own recipe. Play with the ingredients in front of you to devise new and ever more satisfying flavours!

Stuff to try

- Listen to audiobooks where authors read their books aloud. Spoken rhythms you hear amplify words on the page. Record and replay a story extract. Does it affect how you respond to the story? What would you change?

- Look up plagiarism in a dictionary and avoid it.

- Try exploring or writing fan fiction. Afterwards, note what you enjoyed about it. Was anything frustrating for you?

'I have stolen ideas from every book I have ever read.'
- Philip Pullman

Stuff that Works

Know the Audience

When I am writing for other people, I have to know my audience and achieve a near-impossible feat of mind-reading.

Work out early on what it is that will make your book fly off the shelves. Identify the unique selling point. It could be your character's highly original point of view, or that you spent a year shipwrecked on a tiny island and wrote your story based on experience.

These days, I write mostly for children. To keep my writing relevant, I run author events in schools. During these lively sessions I chat to pupils, present my latest books, and give them sneak previews of any work-in-progress. Extracts are read, where I solicit opinions and invite instant feedback. I also encourage schools to send reviews.

If authors underplay or overwork their stories, and make them too simple or complex, it can alienate potential readers, even young ones. Readers, listeners and viewers need to relate to something. Something in the plot, character, message or style.

I tend to begin with a general idea that I think might excite and engage young readers. I write my first draft for me. No one else sees it so I am free to take the plot and characters wherever I wish. After that, I shape it with my audience in mind. I may write ten or twenty drafts before I send my embryonic book to an editor ... who will treat it as a first draft.

Then the really hard work begins.

Stuff to try

- Think back to a novel that you never finished. Can you remember why? How did you feel? Did you put it down to being a mismatch between author and reader?

- Reflect on a book that you were totally immersed in and loved. What was it that drew you in? How did the author tap into your soul?

- Go through any notes for new stories. Take a moment to really reflect on who might like to read your work.

- When you have completed a new story, sit back and imagine who might be reading it. Really visualise them.

- Identify books that match the profile of the one you are writing. Look at where and how they are pitched and who ends up reading them. Your audience will consist of people who find your writing appealing. This might not be the same people that you initially set out to write for. After all, Harry Potter books appeal to adults as well as children.

'No legacy is so rich as honesty.' - William Shakespeare

If It Feels Wrong It Usually Is

Write a book that someone wants to read. One that you also want to write.

Simple advice. Hard to put into practice. All I can say is create the best book you can, and trust yourself and your ability.

Then, when something in your writing is not right, an alarm bell should ring in your head, especially if there is a growing, sense of unease.

It might be about a particular character arc. Maybe your sub-plot isn't flowing as well as you would like? If so ... stop! Give yourself a mundane job for a few minutes. Make a cup of tea. Walk the dog. Empty the bin. Clear the fog and return with a clear head, ready to focus on any niggling issues.

Don't let it lie or unsettle you. Stay detached and sort out the problem in your story; reordering, rewriting or removing elements as necessary.

It is often the case that a writer is holding back too much. A funny book for children is not really that funny. Or a mystery adventure is not actually that mysterious or adventurous. If you are in this position, then there is a solution.

Amplify the message.

Make funny stuff genuinely FUNNY! Don't just thrill, actually THRILL!

Stuff to try

- Have a story that is not working out? Reappraise the main concept or theme. Some ideas are non-starters so lose them and quickly move on.

- Sometimes less is more. Cut out filler words and phrases.

- Children's books occasionally have a wearisome 'look at me! I'm really funny' tone that comes over as desperate. It is better to let readers decide for themselves. See if you can spot books that make big claims but struggle to deliver.

- Cut and paste any troublesome text into an email. Send it to yourself. When you open the document, it will be as if it came from someone else. This approach should help you look at your work more objectively.

Be Like Spock

A senior crew member on the fictional Starship Enterprise, Spock was known for his logical manner. His restrained factual summaries contrasted with the emotional energy of Captain Kirk.

When I worked for an independent television company, I analysed many scripts. I used my knowledge of each show's format to pinpoint any flaws regarding internal logic.

All good stories require well thought through internal logic. Authors must generate a universal set of reasonable and logical rules for the worlds their characters inhabit. This logic applies to forces too. Readers base their expectations and responses on the consistency of your rules. Logic is closely aligned to a story's structure, so ensure the overarching narrative framework makes coherent sense.

In the movie Gremlins, evil Gremlins are killed by sunlight. This structural rule is set up at the start and it would be very unwise to break it. The audience would rightly feel cheated.

Logic will only get you so far. A truly engaging story requires readers to care about the internal struggle your characters are going through. A character might act illogically and do something the reader would never do. But that is okay as long as they learn something from their mistakes. Characters who learn nothing on a journey do not evolve and are inevitably bland.

Even Spock was illogical sometimes. But only when it fitted into the wider story logic. His internal struggle made him, not surprisingly, more human.

Stuff to try

- Look for examples of logical absolutes in stories. Those unbending rules that help explain a world and how characters act within it.

- When assessing the logical progression in a story, ask why X, Y or Z happened. As you read through your drafts, highlight these 'Why?' moments and ensure you have a suitably robust 'Because'.

- A story should solve an unavoidable problem. Create a problem and explore how you would solve it sequentially. Note the emotional changes a character must go through.

- Superman can fly unaided. You and I cannot. He operates under a different set of logical rules to us. Consider how this might affect his world view.

'You do not change people's minds by defeating them with logic.' - Herbert Simon

Play with Expectations

Like many other published writers, I love to subvert expectations.

Consider a story where a scheming adult seeks the fortune of three ill-starred young orphans. The power balance appears to be with the adult but, as the story progresses, it actually is with the children. This is what underpins the narrative of Lemony Snicket's A Series of Unfortunate Events. Lemony Snicket also subverts what we expect of a book's narrator in that he often breaks away from the action to explain how terrible things are going to get. You, as the reader, are brought out of the story for a moment.

Best to be used sparingly, as playing with expectations for the sake of it will break the trust between readers and authors.

Ensure your characters are given sufficient motivation to deserve the cliffhanging moment, or the dramatic twist ending. A satisfying twist comes from the logical set up and unfolding of earlier events. Never from misleading for the sake of it.

Stuff to try

- Reflect on stories that subvert expectations. Blockbuster movies do it on a regular basis. As do crime and thriller stories.

- Acting contrary to an established principle is common in narratives. Characters do it. So can the weather. Readers love to be challenged and surprised. Consider different ways that predictable assumptions or beliefs might be subverted.

- Subverting expectations can be related to a character's mood, professional knowledge, gender. Create a rounded character by considering such elements.

'Sometimes people get mad at The Simpsons' subversive storytelling, but there's another message in there, which is a celebration of making wild, funny stories.'
- Matt Groening

Show Don't Tell

Action is everything, regardless of genre. If your main character has to waffle a page of exposition to explain a plot twist then something is wrong.

While I like characters to hint at their future choices, I avoid them spouting something they know out loud to others just so we can 'overhear' it. All they really need do is convey just enough detail to advance the plot, or further the action.

It is also far better to evoke an emotional response, than to simply recount an event. If characters feel threatened, subtly imply it by describing their tense body language, wary movements and uncertain intent.

Perhaps use short, staccato sentences with menacing ... pauses.

The imagery you create will play out in the minds of readers. Have them make up personal responses to your words.

'She heard the door open and felt scared.'

is less successful at conveying emotion than

'One turn, one creak, of the cold, brass handle set her pulse pounding.'

Words like happy, scared and angry form a speedy, though not very satisfying, way of getting an emotion over. When a character has a particular emotional mood, such as being scared, it is more satisfying to describe the physical reaction. The quickening pulse, trickling sweat, diluted gaze and dry mouth.

Let readers experience what the character is going through in real time. It may help to keep your character 'in the moment'. That way, you can retell the story through a character's eyes!

Stuff to try

- Compile a list of common words that convey emotions and feelings, e.g., jealous, sad, cold. Pick one and explore how it makes you feel mentally and physically.

- Flick through books and collect verbs that clearly convey action.

- Consider which is better: *'Jack was falling.' 'A violent wind battered Jack as he fell.'*

- Waiting for a publisher to respond to a book submission is tense. Nothing beats the feeling of relief and delight when a story is accepted. Tap into these moments of heightened emotion.

'You've got to express yourself in life, and it's better out than in. What you reveal, you heal.' - Chris Martin

Reappraise Rejection

Studies of the brain show that a positive mental attitude releases chemicals to improve one's mood and boost brain power.

Simply smiling as you go about your day will release mood-boosting neurotransmitters like dopamine and serotonin. Also neuropeptides that help influence neural activity.

Staying positive keeps me writing.

I still have several folders full of rejections from my early days as a writer. I am reluctant to throw them out as they are part of a personal journey. It is satisfying to read an earlier rejection and know that I was subsequently published by the same company.

To keep rejections to a minimum, I follow this advice:

Be sure that your work is a good fit for a publisher's house style.

Follow the submission advice to the letter. If it has to be presented typed, double-spaced, in 12 point Courier font then go with that.

Compile a list of publishing contacts, noting each person's title, contact details, and - if known - level of interest.

Often a story may be rejected but the editor likes your style. So send another story and reference the earlier positive response. This approach led me to becoming a freelance writer for Junior Education Magazine.

Follow authors you admire on social media. You are sure to pick up useful tips from their online posts.

Some may respond to direct messages. Don't worry of you don't get a response. Some authors who barely interact online see social media as a necessary evil, as it cuts into valuable writing time.

Stuff to try

- Identify positives from correspondence you have received from publishers. Mull over any constructive criticism. A rejection letter that appears on first glance to be overly-negative, may convey a more positive impression when read later, after a suitable cooling-off period.

- Link up with other authors. Have a chat with them about their experiences.

'When you go through a negative situation, don't think about it. Make it positive.' - Yoko Ono

Better Than It Was

Probably my favourite writing tip. I use it a lot, especially on days when I wonder why I bother to keep writing. Days when my computer has crashed, or a story submission has been rejected.

I have a 'less is more' principle where I take the draft to a certain point, leave it, and then think to myself ... better than it was. That way, I am less tempted to fiddle and overwork initial ideas.

It does not mean I let unfinished writing go. Just that it is okay to take your creative stuff so far, then let it rest. As long as something is better than it was, then progress has been made.

Stuff to try

- Find a piece of writing that successfully accomplished what you were trying to achieve. Relive the pleasurable feeling of having done something well.

- I kept a playscript in a drawer for two years, then rediscovered it and made it better than it was. I sent it to the BBC where it went on to be broadcast. Rediscover an abandoned or forgotten project and give it a polish.

- As you improve as a writer you will create more unfinished pieces. Take a look back at your earlier writing and consider where you could make it better. Use this knowledge to inform your current writing.

'Art is never finished, only abandoned.'
- Leonardo da Vinci

Clarity is Everything

Get the basics right. Be clear about your premise and theme. Know your characters. Place them in clearly defined settings. Nail down their relationships and set the direct of travel.

Every so often, summarise in your mind the plot's past, present and future action.

Ditch wordy descriptions, pretentious sounding words, and instead really focus on what you want to say. Write it. Then mercilessly prune any rambling, overly-complex words and sentences.

Stuff to try

- Avoid nominalisations as they make a sentence less clear. A typical example is a verb masquerading as a noun, usually end in -tion. 'There is an important need for effective communication.' 'It is important to communicate effectively.' Which sentence has greatest clarity?

- Politicians use euphemisms to hide the seriousness of a situation. The term 'collateral damage' masks the enormity of civilian injury and death. A euphemism is only good if it makes sense, though many lack clarity. Flag any you see.

- Repetition is often done for emphasis and stress, yet an over-use of synonyms makes sentences confusing, perplexing, baffling and inexplicable. Observe, detect and notice situations where you repeat, reiterate and replicate yourself.

'Clarity keeps you from boredom.' - Kim Basinger

Value Your Name

I read a famous celebrity's autobiography and the jokes were forced, the dialogue felt flat. I felt short-changed. The celeb lacked the skill to write a well-crafted book. This explains why so many public figures use a ghostwriter.

When a capable writer comes on board, the end result should be more engaging and better received, despite the lack of creative transparency.

Ghostwritten books can also lack a certain intimacy, and fail to credit the ghostwriter which may lead a reader to feel duped if the real author is revealed. Though, I have met ghostwriters who are content to beaver away in the background, provided the money - and the working relationship - is good.

I prefer to have my name on projects. This may not be possible, due to internal politics or writers lacking enough clout to insist on a credit. Be prepared to ask for recognition and push for a say in the final output. Your reputation may depend on it.

Stuff to try

- Look out for celebrity autobiographies. Do any have a shared credit hidden under the cover?

- Reflect on the pros and cons of ghostwriting.

'Never write anything that does not give you great pleasure. Emotion is easily transferred from the writer to the reader.' - Joseph Joubert

Rule of Three

There is something satisfying about events happening in threes.

Omne Trium Perfectum is a Latin phrase that translates as Everything that comes in threes is perfect. It may refer to the fact that things have a beginning, middle and end.

The Rule of Three is a useful device to use when writing comedy. We like patterns. We like surprises. So when a pattern breaks down suddenly it can be very funny. A typical two beat (normal) set-up and one beat (surprising) pay-off.

You can take an unusual situation and make it even wackier. In one of my books for children, animals are unable to move because of fiendish Auntie Hettie's extra sticky hairspray.

The gnus were glued; the iguanas were gummed. Even the ducks were stuck.

Murder Mysteries play on the Rule of Three. One deathly occurrence in a meeting of very old friends is probably expected. Two could be seen as a terrible coincidence. Three? Get out of there!

Stuff to try

- We are tuned into the Rule of Three from an early age, hearing stories about the three little pigs, the three billy goats gruff, Goldilocks and the three bears. Identify more stories that use the Rule of Three.

- Politicians, playwrights, scriptwriters and songwriters often use three words: *Education, Education, Education. Friends, Romans, Countrymen. Make it so.* They act like memorable soundbites. Humans naturally chunk information because it is easier to remember and recall. Look out for other examples.

- Some people believe dramatic events happen in threes, such as when three aeroplanes crash over a short period of time. Logically though, by simply shortening or lengthening the timeframe, the problem disappears. Consider how you can build the Rule of Three into your writing for dramatic effect.

'They took my dressing room, my parking space, even my writers so I don't have a funny third item!'
- Krusty the Clown, The Simpsons

Writing Prompts

Whenever I feel I need a bit of creative inspiration, I browse through my collection of writing prompts and choose one that interests me.

Stuff to try

Writing prompts act as a springboard for the mind. You soar upwards, twisting and turning in all directions, and never know where you will land!

Try the following examples. If a particular prompt doesn't work for you, ditch it quickly and try another. The aim is to get something down, anything.

'You can't wait for inspiration. You have to go after it with a club.' - Jack London

First and Last

First and last experiences are memorable.

Stuff to try

- Explore these first and last prompts.

  My first holiday
  My first sadness
  My first memory
  My first friend
  My first house
  My first kiss
  My last coat.
  My last surprise
  My last argument
  My last cry
  My last treat
  My last hug

- Read the first and last lines in fiction books. Use them to stimulate your own story.

'Nothing can be sadder or more profound than to see a thousand things for the first and last time.' - Victor Hugo

Senses

Sensory prompts promote a different perspective.

Stuff to try

- Choose an easily accessible household object. Explore how it feels.

- Now, if safe to do so, investigate how it smells. Keep moving between all your senses. Do the same with edible items.

- Change your viewpoint. View things around you from a distance. Get up close. Go down low or up high.

- View an object alone, then with others. Discuss what you are seeing. Does anything stand out for you? Do you see anything new?

- Use all your senses to describe a familiar place.

- Now imagine a place that is opposite to it. How do you react to this new, unfamiliar setting?

'Our senses are so many strings that are struck by surrounding objects and that also frequently strike themselves.' - Denis Diderot

Signs

A sign may contain information, a warning or an instruction. Signs prompt us to act in different ways. They can also prompt our writing.

Stuff to try

- Create a simple story from the next sign that you see, e.g. *No Entry.*

- Write a summary. *They couldn't find their way into the old lady's house. Too many boxes overflowing with memories.*

- Create a brief story based on one of these signs:

  Do Not Pass
  Drink Me
  Caution Trip Hazard

- At a suitable point in your next story insert a sign. Perhaps on a bottle, or a gravestone. Use it to send your story in a new direction.

'Life is one big road with lots of signs so when you riding through the ruts, don't complicate your mind.'
- Bob Marley

Conversations

Overheard conversations often provide writers with valuable material.

'Well, it wasn't always as big as that!'
'Did you see that fox on my car roof?'

Stuff to try

- Keep a notebook handy or use a note taking app on your phone. Log memorable conversations you overhear during your day.

- Note some key points about the people involved: age, relationship, clothing, posture, mood, etc.

- Turn one of these conversations into a short story. Does anything change if you alter the setting, or the age of the characters?

- Listen to the conversations around you. Internalise any differences in rhythm, tone and volume.

- Note any words that stand out. Are they local to the area? Or unfamiliar?

- Write a conversation where one person is trying to get the other to admit something personal or incriminating.

- Listen for silences. Identify pauses between words and people. Do those involved interrupt each other? Are they really listening to each other or themselves?

- Think back to a recent conversation that sticks in your mind. What makes it so memorable?

- Have your characters speak about a topic without naming it. Does one have an embarrassing secret?

- Listen to a rambling conversation and sum it up it in your head so you can express the main points.

'Describe character using what the characters see or do or think, but not what they had done or where they had been.' - Colm Toibin

News

I enjoy the way local newspapers like to magnify a trivial situation, or present news with a comic angle.

Elephant Lost In City Park

Man Stole Tweezers

103

Stuff to try

- Read a local paper and note interesting stories. Alter the original headings or sub-headings to make them more dramatic.

- Study the paper's Births, Marriages and Deaths section. Picture the lives of people who are mentioned.

- Identify local phrases. A local Scottish paper near me refers to *'rammies'* (brawls) and *'stooshies'* (arguments).

- News covers the who, what, when, where, why & how something happened. How well do the news articles that you read answer these questions?

'I read the newspaper avidly. It is my one form of continuous fiction.' - Aneurin Bevan

Unexpected Incidents

Life often takes us by surprise. A few years ago while busy writing, I heard a loud crash. I ran outside and saw an upside-down car, its wheels still spinning. The somewhat bemused 90 year old driver was fine, though shaken.

Stuff to try

- Take a recent incident that happened to you and explore it from the perspective of someone much younger or older than you.

- Be playful. React to an unexpected situation. *Today my fence blew down. I am waiting for the wind to blow it back up again.*

- Picture yourself doing a trivial action, such as stepping off a ladder.

- Explore situations where a small action becomes very significant. A boot stepping off a ladder does not seem that important until you realise it is stepping on The Moon!

- Ask people about the most unexpected event that they have experienced.

'Who is going to judge whether my experience of an incident is more valid than yours? No one can be trusted to be the judge of that.' - Tracey Emin

First Lines

The first line of a story must really connect with the reader. One of my favourite first lines was written by Eric Arthur Blair, aka George Orwell.

'It was a bright cold day in April, and the clocks were striking thirteen.' - 1984

It begins with a certain normality that morphs into something quite odd. The line, not yet given any context, sparks interest.

Stuff to try

- Choose one of these sentences as the first line of your next story:

    Drake knew he only had one chance.
    Tomorrow is another pay packet.
    I saw nothing in those cold dead eyes.
    Surely there were more left alive?
    In the end, we all leave.

- Take a book that you have not enjoyed reading and give it a first line make-over.

- Read the blurb on the back of a book. How well does it tie in to the first line of the story? First lines often set the scene or set up a question.

'A line is a dot that went for a walk.' - Paul Klee

Photographs

Though a photograph is a snapshot in time it never gives the whole picture.

Stuff to try

- Invent a family history or potted biography for someone in a photograph you have not met.

- Photographic images on leaflets try to persuade people to think a certain way. Reflect on your response to facial expressions, clothing and body posture.

- Compare a photo of yourself when you were younger to how you appear now, via a newly taken selfie. Identify similarities and differences. Talk to the younger you.

- Collect random images of objects and people. Use them as inspiration. Invent equally random backstories.

- Find photos of you with other children. What conversations can you remember from your childhood?

- Study old photographs for small details. Is there a dog off the lead in the background? Create a major narrative from such minor details.

'I love the people I photograph. I mean, they're my friends. I've never met most of them or I don't know them at all, yet through my images I live with them.'
- Bruce Gilden

Memories

Momentous events create unforgettable memories. My earliest memory is sitting in front of a small black and white television set, watching astronauts land on the Moon.

Stuff to try

- Looking around, choose a section of the room you are in or part of an outside space. Close your eyes for a moment. Can you visualise what you have just seen? Seek out small details and colours. Push your recall hard.

- Take a distant childhood memory. Write about the weather, the temperature, any tastes and smells. Bring all the senses into play. Show your writing to someone who was also there. How similar are your memories?

- Describe three things about a childhood friend that made this person special to you.

- Reflect on how memories are portrayed in different mediums.

- Recall a family custom or tradition. Note any emotions this memory evokes. I happily remember the ever-present jelly trifle at family gatherings.

'To an old memory like mine the present days are but as a little water poured on the deep.' - George Eliot

'There are some things one remembers even though they may never have happened.' - Harold Pinter

Summing Up All That Stuff

Life is a big distraction. There are so many interesting things other than writing to be getting on with, which brings me back to the start of the book. *What are your reasons for writing?* Only you will know. Only you can bring the required passion and commitment to your work. Only you can continue writing.

You never know, you might surprise yourself. And get a book deal! Or, at the very least, a lot of satisfaction.

'Whatever you can do, or dream you can, begin it; boldness has genius, power and magic in it.' - Goethe

Selected Works by Alan Dapré

STAGE
Comeback

RADIO
Kenny
Stranger in the Home
Ulrik the Skiing Viking
The Chariot Race

TELEVISION
Brum x10 *Boohbah* x 43
Blips x 23 *Tronji* x 29

TV TIE-IN TITLES
Brum x 28 *Boohbah* x 8

PUBLISHED PLAYS
The Boss *Another Level*
Timeship *Beware the Wolf* *The Finders*

PICTURE BOOKS
Amy's Armbands *Beanpole Billy*
Grizzly Ben

CHAPTER BOOKS
The Mint Choc Touch / The Monster Maze
Porridge The Tartan Cat:
Brawsome Bagpipes *Bash-Crash-Ding*
KIttycat Kidnap *Loch Ness Mess*
Unfair Funfair *Pet Show Show-Off*

Printed in Great Britain
by Amazon

23345197R00066